El Jireh

The God Who Provides

Compiled by
Living Parables of Central Florida

El Jireh

The God Who Provides

ISBN 978-1-963611-60-1

Cover Design: Robin Black

All interior images by https://www.freepik.com/GodProvides

Published by EA Books Publishing a division of
Living Parables of Central Florida, Inc. a 501c3
EABooksPublishing.com

ACKNOWLEDGMENTS

We thank Cheri Cowell and her wonderful team at EABooks Publishing for giving us this opportunity and our many friends and family for supporting us in our writing dreams. And most importantly, we want to thank our Lord and Savior Jesus Christ for His gifts—may this book bring you the honor and glory you deserve.

TABLE OF CONTENTS

NOTE FROM THE PUBLISHER

It is a daunting thing to submit your writing to a publisher. Doubts and fears prevent many from following their dream of becoming a published author. But these brave souls persevered. They overcame those doubts and fears, and they submitted. Then they waited. Those chosen for inclusion have followed their dream, submitted to the process, and are now published authors. We are proud of them and are grateful you've joined them in celebrating this milestone. May you find a reminder that God is also your El Jireh in their writings.

El Jireh

The God Who Provides

Compiled by
Living Parables of Central Florida

When God Shows Up

Nancy Kay Grace

My thoughts swirled. Sleep escaped me. Hours passed.

Worry didn't keep me awake; my insomnia arose from happiness. A new possibility had opened to help me deal with the sadness of separation from my grandchildren. Several years prior, my husband, Rick, and I had moved further away from our family so he could serve in a ministry position. Now, he had been permitted by his governing board to work remotely if we wanted to relocate closer to family. That meant moving a thousand miles from Illinois to Texas. I felt excited at the thought of living near our four grandchildren and hours closer to two other grands.

Rick and I prayed for nearly two years, waiting for God to provide a home closer to our family. We house hunted every time we visited Texas, contacting realtors and visiting new subdivisions. The more we looked, the more discouraged we became. Housing prices in the area were higher than we could afford, and mortgage interest rates rose. The possibility of moving closer to our grandchildren diminished due to lack of affordability.

I knew we didn't have to move. I would be content where we were, although it was far from grandchildren's hugs. God had provided good friends for us where we lived. However, I felt sad seeing my friends often connecting with their grandchildren, especially on holidays and birthdays. Visiting our grandchildren involved planning and days of travel. I longed to see their smiles and hear their laughter.

We sought the Lord together in prayer. We didn't want to rush ahead of God and take on debt from a house we couldn't afford in our retirement years. The possibility of our relocation grew dimmer. Would God provide an appropriate living space for us?

One of the hardest parts of prayer is waiting. As believers we learn to petition God for our needs, but we get anxious when the answer is slow in coming. We wonder if he heard us, or if we're being selfish. We feel the tension between knowing God will provide the answer and feeling frustrated while we wait. Discouragement clouds our hope. Those emotions surfaced as we believed God would make a way, as we prayed . . . and waited.

On one of our early house-hunting visits, I signed up on an email list for a developer, more out of curiosity than anything.

In mid-December, we planned to visit our Texans. Before our trip, I got an email from the developer about a house they wanted to sell by the end of the year, with a huge price reduction to sell on a certain weekend. The possibility seemed far-fetched that we could buy a brand-new home with the rising costs.

On Friday night of our visit, we talked with our son and his wife, expressing our uncertainty about our ability to relocate. They admitted they'd given up hope. Together, we settled into the disappointment of that possibility. We surrendered the situation to God.

The next morning, Rick and I had an appointment to see the house mentioned in the email. We toured it while thinking that we could not afford the new house.

The agent explained the price reduction because the company wanted to sell it that weekend. The lower cost put the house within our price range. The developer also offered lower mortgage rates and significant help with closing costs.

Rick and I walked through the house one last time, pausing to pray in the living room. We needed God's guidance for this big decision. Was this God's provision to move us closer to our family for the next season of life?

Peace settled over us.

Back at the agent's desk, she asked about our decision. With joy and gratitude, we stated we'd purchase the home.

After signing all the paperwork, we took a picture of ourselves with big smiles in front of the house, holding a sign with the words, "I saw it, I liked it, I bought it!"

We returned to our son's home, restraining our joy.

"How did it go?" he asked.

We didn't say anything but showed him the photo on my phone.

His jaw dropped. We would soon be living close enough for soccer games and school programs and most importantly, for grandparenting.

God continued to bring together all the pieces of our move. Our house sold in Illinois without being listed with a realtor. We downsized and prepared to move in two months.

The biggest lesson we learned was that when we gave up, God showed up.

God provided the right timing—an email about a house we could tour while we were in Texas. We were the first ones in line to see the house, with many couples behind us.

God provided our physical and family needs—the house was the right price and size and was within an hour of our family. Also, we would be hours closer to our other grandchildren, making the drive to their house doable. We could invest more in the lives of the next generation.

As Christ's followers, we pray and wait for God to answer. We wonder how he will supply. And then, when God answers, we are often surprised.

After we moved, a new acquaintance gave me a decorative wooden sign with the words, "I still remember the days I prayed for the things I have now."

Yes. I smiled with gratitude. That person could not have known how appropriate it was.

I sleep in peace in our new home, remembering how God provides in unanticipated ways.

Nancy Kay Grace is a speaker, writing coach, and author of *The Grace Impact*. She writes about hope, God's grace, and perseverance as a cancer survivor: her website and *GraceNotes* newsletter sign-up at www.nancykaygrace.com. For relaxation, Nancy enjoys hugs from grandchildren, playing worship songs on the piano, and traveling.

He Leads Me Beside Still Waters

Julie R. Greenwalt

It's true: Sailing is about the journey. Catalina Island, off the California coast, is only twenty-six miles from Long Beach Harbor, an hour by ferry or just 15 minutes by helicopter. But for us sailors, even with favorable winds and if we could sail in a straight line, six hours to the island is making *good time.*

We enjoyed perfect weather on this trip, one of our first to Catalina. I was enchanted by the boat's rhythm, steering by tiller (my first time to "drive"), and especially watching dolphins jumping around the boat. My husband, Roger, dozed in the cockpit while I stared around at the wonders of the sea. Everything he promised me about this voyage was coming true.

Watching newbie sailors try to attach their boats to a floating harbor mooring ball is a great source of entertainment for fellow sailors and onlookers from nearby shores and docks. The trick is to grab the tall wand floating upright next to your assigned mooring, pull it aboard, then quickly attach the rope from the wand to boat cleats at the front (bow) and stern (back) of the boat, all the while keeping the boat from drifting sideways into the boat next door. Sometimes, shouting from bow to stern or boat to boat is involved. But on this perfect trip, we connected our tiny sailboat properly on the first try.

Grabbing duffle bags, we climbed aboard a water taxi, feeling like seasoned veterans. Our twenty-five foot boat wasn't equipped with adequate sleeping quarters or other amenities, so we'd splurged on a boutique hotel up the hill.

The next morning, it was another gorgeous day aboard our little boat. We chatted with the harbor master before casting off. It was a helpful and informative conversation until his parting words. As he looked over our slightly dilapidated thirty year-old boat, he offered this farewell: "Better you than me."

Good grief, I wanted to dive overboard and buy a ticket on the next ferry home. Our boat was unfit for sailing, and we didn't even know it.

"Roger—" I began.

"No, Julie," he interrupted before I could get started. "The harbor master knows nothing about our skill level, training, or experience. And—by the way—didn't we sail over safely yesterday? Our boat is seaworthy, and we know what we're doing."

But I was willing, at that moment, to take the harbor master's word for it that if we dared leave the safety of the harbor that day, we were doomed.

After I calmed down, we motored slowly toward the harbor entrance. Back then, we used a hand-held GPS for guidance, and I thought it would be fun to see which of us had a better sense of direction, so I asked Roger, "Which way is home?" He pointed to the left, and I pointed to the right. But the GPS pointed somewhere in the middle. Surely it was malfunctioning. Maybe the batteries were weak, or a solar storm affected its accuracy. Even though we were both convinced it was wrong, we finally agreed to trust the GPS until we could see landmarks to correct our course. The GPS steered us straight back to the boat ramp we started from in Long Beach Harbor.

"Roger, I know there's a big rock, but I can't see it!" I shouted frantically, straining to see beyond the bow of our sailboat. This time, we were aboard our second boat, *Wandering Spirit*. She was thirty-six feet long, complete with beds, a galley (kitchen), and a head (bathroom) with a shower—pure luxury compared to our first little sailboat. Frenchy's Cove on Anacapa Island was a familiar anchoring spot, but we usually arrived early enough to navigate with our eyes around the rock. Now, the nighttime shadows cast by the island blocked all light, in contrast to the brightly lit coastline of California at our backs. The recently purchased spotlight I held in one hand wasn't strong enough to penetrate more than ten feet of blackness, and of course, a boat can't stop on a dime. I grabbed the lifeline, certain that *Wandering Spirit* was about to crunch into that rock and go down like the *Titanic*.

"Julie, I've got the GPS—I can see the rock. We're not going to hit it; don't worry!" Roger called back from the helm. I was still gasping, light-headed with fear as *Wandering Spirit* slowly plowed forward. Even after the anchor splashed into shallow water, my breathing didn't return to normal for several minutes.

Another day, at another island, we dropped anchor in a calm bay one sunny afternoon. By now, we were well-seasoned sailors, accustomed to dealing with all kinds of boat malfunctions, weather conditions, and seasickness. This two-day trip was special because our son-in-law and daughter were aboard one month before their first child (and our first grandchild) was due. I'm here to tell you that nothing tastes as good as salmon barbequed on a sailboat with a nice salad on the side. We played games until bedtime, and then Roger and I climbed into our V-shaped bunk in the boat's bow while the other two bedded down on the converted table.

Deep in the night, a loud grinding beside my head jolted us awake. I screamed (so helpful in an emergency), even as Roger shouted for everyone to stay calm until we could figure out what had happened. We scrambled up on deck and were confused to find *Wandering Spirit* bumping against a rocky cliff and the anchor rope floating in the water. It had separated from the anchor chain and our anchor was now unattached on the ocean floor, leaving our sailboat to float freely.

Thankfully, the current took the boat toward the island instead of away from it and out into the busy shipping lanes, where we might not have awakened until disaster struck. Still, with no anchor and no damage to the hull, we had no choice but to get dressed and sail through the night back to the coast.

I was downcast without knowing why for several days after the anchor incident. Finally, I realized I was experiencing a delayed reaction. What was I thinking, to take our eight-months-pregnant daughter out on the boat, especially overnight and far from ambulances and doctors? Even though nothing disastrous happened, what if it had? I felt deeply irresponsible, a failure as a grandmother before I even became one.

Who wouldn't be afraid when you can't see the rock you're sure is waiting to wreck you? Who wouldn't scream when the boat you thought was safely anchored crashed into an island in the middle of the night? Who wouldn't be concerned about a negative assessment of their sailboat by an experienced harbor master?

Oh, how I enjoy the times our sailing journey, like our life, is full of wonder, without unplanned-for disasters. Yet our infallible harbor master, Jesus, was with us in the "better you than me" boat at Catalina Island, and He was in the boat when our anchor let go — just as He was with His disciples in their boat on the stormy Sea of Galilee.

Rocks, lost anchors, and potentially faulty navigational systems are not frightening or surprising to Jesus. He is not upset or disappointed when I scream from fright; He only reminds me that He is beside me, offering comfort and providing peace no matter what happens. And He promised to always be with me, to show me the way.

We love having friends and family join us on our sailing journeys, and we enjoy asking our visitors, "What's the difference between an adventure and an ordeal?"

The answer? Your attitude. When I choose to fix my eyes on Jesus, my attitude stems from the sense of security He gives.

The best moment of every sailing trip is when we pass into the safe, still waters of the harbor, whether at an island or our home slip. The waves smooth out, the boat stops heeling, and we begin furling the sails and prepping the boat for the journey's end. *Wandering Spirit* slides gently into the dock; we snap on her sail covers, hose her down, grab our overnight gear, and walk up the dock to our waiting car. Our El Jireh always provides a way to bring our wandering spirits safely home.

Julie Greenwalt is a veteran women's small group facilitator and pastor's wife who has ministered to women in various ways for more than thirty years. She and her husband, Roger, have been married for over forty adventurous years, moving from motorcycles to sailing to full-time RV life and traveling internationally.

Therefore do not be anxious, saying, 'What shall we eat?' or 'What shall we drink?' or 'What shall we wear?' For the Gentiles seek after all these things, and your heavenly Father knows that you need them all.

— Matthew 6:31-32, ESV

Wrapped in Common Swaddle

Barbara Taylor Wright

But my God shall supply all your need, according to
His riches in Christ Jesus.
Philippians 4:19, KJV

I often ponder how the Jewish sages missed the coming of the Messiah. Maybe they expected a much grander entrance with nothing of the ordinary. He came quietly and announced to only a chosen few. No palace. His first cries bounced off the stone walls of a cave. No rich robes and crowns. He was wrapped in the common swaddling.

Too often, the miracle of answered prayer comes wrapped in the common swaddling—the ordinary moments of ordinary days. How many times do we fail to see the miraculous? We chalk up God's provision to chance and coincidence, and just like the Jewish sages of old, we miss Him.

Two weeks before Christmas in 1984, our little family left our ministry in Montana to go across several states to visit family. The snow began as we made our way in our faithful little car. With no working radio and, in 1984, no cell phone, we grew worried. The highway was whiting out, and traffic was sparse—even the huge eighteen wheelers had disappeared.

Then it happened, that awful sound under the hood. The car began to lose power. My husband, Randy, spotted an exit sign through the blizzard. Our car jerked and sputtered off the highway, and we rolled into a hotel parking lot.

We carried less than one hundred dollars in our pockets. We calculated just enough to buy gas to get us home. A neon sign announced that a room was $49, so having no other option, we checked in.

When we peeked out the window the next morning, snow covered the world like a fluffy white blanket. Our car was buried to the roof in the parking lot, but by midmorning, the snowplows had done their magic. We ventured outside, and Randy scraped the piled snow from the car, cracked the door loose, and turned the key.

Not a sound.

Not a burp.

Our faithful little car was dead.

The situation was dire. We had less than $50 to our name. We had served in donation-supported mission work for the past few years and lived on just enough, with no padding for a snowy day. We had left the only people we knew west of the Mississippi hundreds of miles back in Montana. Our family and friends were thousands of miles away in South Carolina. What would we do?

Randy found the hotel manager and learned there was a garage a mile down the road.

Always the protector, he kissed me, bundled up, and started hiking. As I watched him disappear over the hill, my heart clenched. What would we do here in the middle of nowhere with no one to call or rescue us?

No One to rescue you? Child, I never leave nor forsake. Trust me.

His voice spoke deep in my heart. I almost didn't want to hear it. I would almost rather wallow in self-pity. How could He rescue me here? There literally would be no room in the inn tonight. We didn't have enough to cover another night at the hotel. There was no one to save us. No one.

I could almost hear the twinkle in His voice.

But I bring you tidings of great joy — unto you is born a Savior.

I sat in the hotel lobby, bouncing our daughter, Melody, on my knee, watching the lights blink on the Christmas tree. I looked at the stunning scenery out the window. The fields were covered in a white blanket of snow. The limbs of the trees bent as if in worship, iced in snowy wonder. A crackly radio spouted out local news, filled in with intermittent Christmas music.

Moment by moment, my heart grew as cold as the wind seeping through the door. I was wrestling with my heart's question: Could He save this time? No one was here who knew or cared about us. How would even He work this out?

I must have looked miserable, because the young girl with a Santa hat behind the counter came across the room and handed me an empty Styrofoam cup. "Miss, you are welcome to some hot cider. Everything is going to be okay."

I wanted to laugh. I wanted to cry—everything will be okay? I took the cup and poured some hot cider as the crackly music from the radio drifted to my ears. "Yet in thy dark streets shineth, the everlasting light. The hopes and fears of all the years are met in thee tonight."

Your hopes, My daughter. Your fears. Met in Him. My Son, sent for you.

"Oh, Father, I want to believe. Help my unbelief," I whispered.

An hour later, a loud tow truck pulled up in the hotel lot. Of all the people, out popped Randy with a small smile. After hearing our story, the garage owner agreed to send his tow truck and have a look at our car. Our little family tucked themselves inside the loud truck with the jolly man and went to wait for a, hopefully, easy fix.

I sat in the cool office that smelled of grease and gasoline and watched Melody play around the coffee table when the mechanic came back in. I could read bad news in his face before he spoke. The engine in our little car was completely gone. He could order parts and fix it, but because of the biggest blizzard in the history of Wyoming, roads were still treacherous, deliveries were delayed, and on top of that, it was Saturday. It would be Monday or Tuesday until the parts were in. He would need one hundred dollars to order the parts; the total was nearly five hundred.

Randy told him our parents would have to wire the money. All we had was $49. Pulling out the wrinkled tens and ones, Randy offered him the last of our money.

Good tidings of great joy. A savior sent for you.

The gentleman excused himself and left the room. I couldn't believe my ears. Tuesday? That was four days away. We had a baby depending on us and nowhere to go. I suddenly understood what Mary must have felt waiting on the donkey as Joseph knocked on door after door.

"The hopes and fears of all the years are met in thee tonight." *Fear not, dear one.*

The mechanic came back in, his face alight with excitement. "Okay, kids," he said, "My wife and I have prayed, and if you'll take it, we would like you to stay in our spare room while we get you back on the road. I spoke to my parts place, and they will send the parts on, and you can pay the whole bill when I get them."

Glory to God in the highest. Peace, goodwill to men — to us.

I wanted to cry. I wanted to dance. "Thank you. Thank you," we said over and over.

And what a wonderful four days followed. Just like Mary and Joseph, we were surrounded by angels sent by God to care for us. Theirs was a modest ranch-style brick home in a snow-covered community, but to me, it was a mansion. To me, it was a miracle. We were loved and cared for. We spent four magical days looking at the snow-covered landscape and marveling at the provision of our Savior King.

Our parents sent the funds to pay for repairs. As we prepared to leave, we embraced our newly found friends with tears and thankful hearts. The car hummed better than it had ever hummed before. It was new.

But so was I. Something happened in that blizzard that could not have happened if we had never been stranded. I had learned to see the miracle — to trust our God. Miracles — a hotel just the right distance to roll into. A young girl behind a desk with an encouraging word and a cup of hot cider. A common mechanic who was anything but common — a king's man in disguise who offered us shelter and food and who God used to build our faith in miracles for years to come. His beautiful wife so full of love and wisdom, caring for us with tenderness and generosity. What were the chances of all of that coming into place? Chance? Oh, I don't think so — his provision wrapped in the common swaddle — just like the greatest gift of His Son.

I could hear the voice of the King as we pulled onto the now-plowed interstate.

I love you. I always make a way. I bring good news — a Savior — born to YOU. You will still find Him today, wrapped in common swaddling.

Prayer: O Lord, Open the eyes of my heart to see Your miraculous provision. Help me to recognize Your answers in the common swaddle of my everyday moments.

Barbara Wright is a seventy-year-old Jesus Movement convert. She holds a BAA in sociology from the University of SC. Barbara worked in social services from 1977–2020. She lives in SC, enjoying her grandchildren and her Frenchie friend, Rollo.

God Provides Through Childhood Cancer

Hannah J. Taylor

God provided temporary supernatural strength to Elijah so he could outrun a chariot. First Kings 18:44–46 says that Elijah ran thirteen miles ahead of Ahab's chariot and beat him to Jezreel. I don't know about you, but I couldn't just up and run thirteen miles, much less faster than a chariot! A chariot could go as fast as 40 miles per hour!

Then, God sent an angel with food and water to Elijah. God provided for Elijah's physical needs for his forty days of hiding! Not just cold sandwiches or a can of something, though. First Kings 19:6 says the cake "was baked on hot stones." God provided food, encouragement, and space to recover and rest. Why did God do this?

Well, God worked through Elijah for the rest of his life. He used Elijah to prophesize and anoint the kings of Israel and Syria. Elijah faithfully did what God told him to do for the remainder of his days. Perhaps one of the greatest things was that through God working in Elijah's life, God made Ahab repent.

Like Elijah, my family is facing a scary enemy. We are fighting a Leukemia battle with our four-year-old daughter, trying to faithfully do what God wants us to do.

The problem started when my daughter and I were with friends at the playground several years ago. While playing, she fell down three stairs and started screaming. She couldn't walk, and her ankle was bruised and swollen, so we headed to an urgent care clinic that had an X-ray machine.

My child's first broken bone, but we adjusted and thought she would heal within weeks. She didn't even need a cast.

A couple of days later, she started running a fever. We followed up with the pediatrician, and he thought she picked up an illness in urgent care. The fever went away the next day. She started running a high fever a few days later, so I called the pediatrician. The fever was gone the next day, so they weren't worried about it. A couple of days later, the fever was higher than ever. Back to the pediatrician, we went. Her pediatrician kindly suggested we go to the ER for a blood draw and urine test. There, we found out that she had high-risk leukemia and would need surgery to place a port and start chemo right away.

Like He did for Elijah, God has provided every need for us. Meals, change for vending machines at the hospital, a neighbor collecting mail and packages, animal care, lawn care, money to buy medical supplies that insurance won't cover, house cleaning, coffee, encouragement, companionship, and prayers. God provided a pediatrician who wisely got us to the hospital quickly, without alarming us with the possibilities, and gave us the best oncology team we could ask for.

God provided for us through family, friends, and church family. We are so grateful to have all these things lifted off our shoulders. Our God truly is greater than any other, our Provider, El Jirah!

Hannah Taylor holds a bachelor's degree in Secondary Education from Clemson University and a master's degree in education from Anderson University. She writes about teaching teens and adults time management.

Website: https://hannahjtaylor.com/
Instagram: @Hannah.Jones.Taylor
Substack: https://substack.com/@hannahjtaylor

Every good gift and every perfect gift is from above,

coming down from the Father of lights, with whom there

is no variation or shadow due to change.

— James 1:17, NIV

Bring the Rain

Darcy Hicks

*If you follow my statutes and faithfully observe
my commands, I will give you rain at the right time,
and the land will yield its produce, and the trees of the
field will bear their fruit.*
Leviticus 26:3-4, CSB

I recently attended a conference where the beautiful lake and sunny weather provided the perfect setting for daily walking. One day, as I went for a stroll around the lake, clouds emerged and the forecast included rain. Looking up at the gray skies, I said, "Lord, I don't want it to rain. It's been so beautiful, and the rain will make it gloomy."

I immediately felt a quickening in my spirit from the Lord. He prompted my heart with that still small voice, "Sometimes you need the rain to wash away the old and nourish the ground so new things can blossom." At that moment, I knew God was providing what I needed and not what I wanted.

Like many of us, I'm not too fond of the rain. It brings dark clouds, stormy weather, and squishy shoes. As far as I am concerned, those dreary days are best for curling up with a good book and taking a nap. As a Florida girl, I prefer bright sunshine and blue skies to rain jackets and umbrellas.

The same goes for our daily lives. We often want them to be picture-perfect and smooth sailing instead of including storm clouds and rough waters wreaking havoc on our plans. But to be well-watered and flourishing, we must welcome the rain and endure dark days. These seasons remind us that only Jesus can quench our thirst for life and calm the storms.

Before that walk, I had been praying for God to change some difficult circumstances in my life, and He used that simple moment to remind me that rainy days are necessary to bring new growth. In the end, God provided for me that morning. The sun emerged from behind the clouds for another lovely day, giving me a new perspective on the rain. I now pray that God provides the rain when needed so old things can be washed away to make way for new life.

Father, please bring the rain at just the right time to the areas of our lives that need watering. Let the storms draw us near you, and may you continue to provide water for the soil of our circumstances so we can bloom for your glory. Amen.

Darcy Hicks lives in Northwest Florida with her husband and children. She encourages others in their faith through writing and speaking. Connect with Darcy through her blog at darcyhicks.com.

Lost and Found

Melody M. Morrison

"I am not afraid," she said. Hands tremble, nails bitten.
"I can do this," she said. Knees throb, heart smitten.
"I don't know the way but I think I can find it."
It cannot be harder than how she lives now.

"Why am I alone with people around me?"
She strains to avoid that pit of despair.
She looks for a respite. "Is it above me?
Or is that what I'm seeing just over there?

"Where can I go to escape this chasm?"
She reaches to brace and stabilize rising.
"How long will I look?" legs in a spasm.
"The view is so bleak, I see nothing surprising?"

Day to day numbs her. "My heart weighs like lead."
Scars etch the pictures engraved in her head.

"All I remember from childhood till now
Is losing the people I wanted somehow.
And yet it is me who has disappeared.
I've tried everything, ending up seared.

"So who was I meant to be? Is there a plan?"
It seems she is constantly taking a stand
For something or someone or nothing at all.
"I am afraid in the end I will fall."

"What do faith and morals matter?
What's the hype in all this chatter.
How can the answer rely on me seeing
That life's too hard for a human being?
My mind's live streaming, constantly buff'ring.
I am afraid that it's all for nothing."

Is it too much to hope to be seen,
To be known by heart, mind, and in between?
Are we so absorbed in "Who am I?"
That we can't afford a look to the sky?

"It's dark inside, and I need some light.
I shouldn't weep over sensing a slight."
Everyone's journey looms equally hard.
But lost ones choose feeling alone with no guard.

An interesting choice to focus on history
Where some things are clear, others a mystery.
And yet, there are ancient and powerful words
With proof from all eras, these improve our world.

Every day gives us twenty-four hours.
We eat and sleep and take our showers.
That's ten or twelve, so where's the rest?
Wallowing, groveling in our own mess?

Where do we find the truth that we seek?
We want to be strong but know we are weak.
Looking at self is just introspection.
"What if I look in another direction?"

The easiest mantra to make a soul whole
Is found in the ancient writings of old.
Love God and love people, for this life is fast.
The healthy look forward, let go of the past.

But you can't love others and not love yourself.
Is that a conundrum we place on a shelf?
The truth is we each hold equivalent value.
But purpose is found when someone will *see* you.

One day you look up and find it is true

That someone forgotten is still there for you.

When you need some honesty, courage, or lift

The Best Friend is near us and offers that gift.

It may be material, or spiritual, or wisdom.

It may be some laughter — escaping the humdrum.

But we should all listen and share what we know.

Humans have limits: we reap what we sow.

Perhaps she will see there's a Source who provides...

He's there if we seek Him. God never hides.

Melody enjoys spending time with her family. She thrives on encouraging people through words and music, so they can recognize their own value and the power of God's Spirit to provide their life's design. God's gifts are unfathomable.

God in the Wagon

Brenda Sue Bynum

Daddy always kept his farm wagon by the smokehouse when he wasn't using it, down by the garden's edge. Daddy hauled hay in his handmade wagon and fetched newborn calves to the barn.

From inside the wagon, you could peek between the cracks of the sideboards and see everything happening in the backyard. Like a bug hiding under the rug, I could lie still, watching my brothers smoke behind the smokehouse, hear their secrets, and count the silly crows flying overhead. Once, I saw a hawk dive for one of our chickens. But some days, it was my hiding place — my refuge.

This day was one of those days. Hot tears streamed down my face uncontrollably. In Daddy's wagon, my favorite place in the world, and right in front of God, my seven-year-old soul poured out all my angst. What a painful end to my unbelievable day at school!

Earlier that morning, on the way to catch the school bus, I'd stepped over all the mud puddles — except one. I knew my teacher would scold me for dragging mud into the classroom again. Wild onion breath and sweet clover hung in the warm, sticky air as my older sister and I walked by the field Daddy had cut the day before. By dawn's light, the outline of Daddy's farm wagon emerged by the fence gate. That wagon would be behind the house by the end of the day.

Sunbeams streaked through the tall oaks behind our farmhouse — a fine day for skipping school and running through the open field to the creek. But I wanted to wear my new dress. Mama had made the beautiful, blue–printed dress with her own hands. Blue, like the sky, was my favorite. I could hardly wait to wear it. Today was the day.

Still, those frogs down by the creek were calling my name. But the brown paper tablet and number four pencil waiting on my desk at school called louder, as I watched the yellow bus cross the bridge.

The screechy bus door closed as I shuffled down the aisle and scooted onto the seat. Giggles and laughter erupted from behind my seat, "She's wearing a flour sack dress!" One girl sneered. I wanted to disappear under the seat. I squirmed, knocking the mud off my shoe until the girls got off the bus.

In the early sixties, when our school days began with the Pledge of Allegiance and morning prayer, I sometimes felt goosebumps as we honored America's flag and the Bible.

I knew about prayer because Mama prayed from her bed at night. I heard her call our names to God, asking Him to keep us safe. I often caught Mama sitting on the couch with her Bible and hands folded, thanking God for her family. Sometimes I wanted to pray, too, but I didn't know what to say.

Then, Ms. Rush wrote our assignment on the blackboard: *Write a row of each alphabet letter.*

By lunch, my paper looked like a smeared mess and my w was wrong. *And why do little kids have to use big, chubby pencils?* That fat, red pencil, without an eraser, rubbed a knot right on my third finger. I licked the tip of my finger and rubbed that silly w until I made a hole. *At home, Mama has a pencil with an eraser. Why can't we use a smaller pencil like Mama's, with a pink eraser on the top? Anyway, my letters never look like the teacher's neatly written letters. If only I had another sheet of paper, but this is my last one.*

I managed to squeeze the rest of the w row around the hole. I guessed that would be all right. After lunch, the class finished the assignment just in time for afternoon recess.

On my way out of the restroom, before class started, the girl on the school bus who had made fun of my dress pressed me against the wall, making my head hit the wall with a thud. She beat my arm with her fist. She whispered in my ear, "I'm showing these girls how tough I am, so they won't bother me. Got it?"

If only I had skipped school that morning, I could have caught minnows and watched the smelly cows chew grass.

I burst into tears and crumpled on the floor. There I sat, sobbing, until the last bell rang for home. With swollen eyes and a damp dress, I ran straight to the bus and got on first so no one would see me. On the ride home, my head hurt, and my arm ached like a bumblebee sting. *Do the field mice feel like this when our cat drags them to the back porch?*

It seemed like forever before the screechy bus door opened. Down the steps and up the drive, I raced. This time, I stomped every mud puddle with a splat!

The back door slammed behind me as I raced through the kitchen, but I stopped dead still when I heard an unfamiliar voice from the living room. I eased to the door, leaned against it, and peeked around the side. A strange lady sat beside Mama on our couch. The lady looked at a piece of paper and said, "I'm afraid some of your children may be taken to foster care."

Taken? Is somebody going to take us away from Mama? The fear I'd had from the bully at school was nothing compared to this! Like Mama chasing the cat to the door, I dashed down the back steps. I fixed my eyes on Daddy's farm wagon, my refuge, at the edge of the backyard and raced for it. I climbed inside and lay flat on my back like I'd done before. Although I had bawled earlier, there was enough to pour out again. *What can I do? I don't want somebody to take us away! I know it's because Daddy is drinking again. He left to find more whiskey; we don't know where he is.*

Daddy drank because his daddy had given him homemade moonshine when he was young. Drinking, to Daddy, was as natural as scratching your head, I suppose. But Daddy's calloused hands and farmer's tan proved his love for his family.

"God," I cried. "Please take me to heaven."

I knew God was in His heaven, for Mama's big Bible, which sat on our coffee table, said so. Mama often told us that God was looking down from heaven. I figured He was waiting for us to talk to Him.

In our living room, above the couch, Mama had hung a picture of an angel helping children cross a shabby bridge with the water raging below. But this was a time I needed to go straight to God without the help of an angel.

I gazed straight up to the sky this time and cried again, "God, please take me to heaven."

As I watched a cottony cloud cover the sun, an unexplainable peace settled over my tense body. I didn't hear a clear voice or see anyone, but my tears stopped, and I felt everything was going to be alright.

Did God see me in the wagon and hear me? I believe He did!

My day of turbulent fear seemed to slither away. Sweet rays of confidence surrounded my child-heart. I knew that Mama would pray that old "foster care" thing away! God must have heard, because we never heard of it again.

From that day on, I knew God was watching over me. Even when I fell in the creek's muddy water and tumbled off the top of the barn.

Although time produced more heartaches, that day in the wagon became a stabilizing memory. For it was there that God's presence steadied my soul. God provides a way for His children, even when there seems to be no way out of a dark situation. God heard the cry of my seven-year-old heart and provided His peaceful assurance that He would always be with me.

The reassurance that He had heard me became a powerful confirmation that He will always hear when I call Him. I learned that when we call upon God from a humble heart, He will meet us anywhere, even in a little farm wagon.

Brenda Sue Bynum, author of children's books, loves to incorporate childhood experiences that teach life lessons into her books. All her books were inspired by humble heroes who impacted her life with the light of God's love. Brendasuebynum.com

Hold on to Hope

Debra Kornfield

After her first intestinal transplant in August 2004, our daughter Karis, twenty-one and an honor student at Notre Dame, went into rejection. Four weeks of treatment failed. At the same time, a dangerous virus invaded her suffering graft.

For days, Karis balanced precariously on a rejection/infection tightrope. Treatments for these two conditions are opposite. The immune system must be suppressed to prevent or treat rejection. Combatting viral infection, though, requires a strong immune system.

On Tuesday evening, November 2, 2004, Karis started coughing.

On Wednesday evening, while waiting for a CT scan of her intestine, Karis said, "I'm having a little trouble breathing." Her nurse hooked her up to oxygen.

Thursday morning, Karis had an endoscopy to visualize her transplanted intestine from the top. Karis and I chatted cheerfully as we waited for the procedure. I waved and smiled as a nurse whisked her to the operating room.

"See you in about an hour, sweetheart."

An hour later, though, instead of her surgeon walking into the waiting room to tell me all had gone well, a pulmonologist appeared, asking me to sign consent for a bronchoscopy. A scope would be inserted into her lungs, withdrawing fluid for culture. "Don't worry—this will only take a few minutes," he told me.

Two anxious *hours* later, Dr. M, a transplant surgeon, approached. "Let's sit down in the conference room," he said. Only one who has been there can fathom the fear those few words instilled in me.

"Karis has inflammation and fluid in her lungs, and they are very stiff. She's not breathing well, so instead of waking her, we sent her to a ventilator in the ICU"

The surgeon paused to glance at my stunned face. "Also, her intestine looks worse, with many open, bleeding, ulcerated patches. Call your family, and then go to the ICU waiting room. We may be able to let you see Karis briefly. And . . . it might be good for you to make plans, in case . . . Perhaps your pastor could come?"

A wave of shock rolled in. Somehow, I made my calls and then stumbled toward the ICU to meet my pastor. The medical team stepped back to allow us a few precious moments to anoint Karis and pray for her healing. She was barely visible under all the medical paraphernalia, tubes, and lines. As the white and blue coats closed around her again, we retreated to the waiting room to make funeral plans. It all felt distant, surreal.

Our son, Dan, arrived first, driving from New York City to Pittsburgh Thursday evening. News from the ICU went from bad to worse. Antibiotics had no effect. Barely thirty-six hours since Karis's first cough, only an area the size of a fist at the top of each lung remained free of infection.

Friday morning, Dr. M told us they had transferred Karis from a ventilator to an oscillator. The oscillator shook Karis's body to force oxygen into her lungs. It only worked if they propped her in one specific position. If they turned her at all, her oxygen level plummeted. The constant shaking of her body made every part of her care more difficult.

Dan left to meet his sister, Rachel's, flight from Chicago. I called my husband, Dave, who was in Brazil, where we were living at the time, with an update. He and our youngest daughter, Valerie, would fly overnight from São

Paulo to Newark and arrive in Pittsburgh late Saturday morning.

Friday afternoon, Dr. M offered Dan, Rachel, and me a flicker of hope. He reviewed Karis's situation for Rachel, including details Dan and I hadn't heard. The day before, while Karis had undergone endoscopy, transplant surgeons had reviewed images of her intestine from the previous evening's CT. It had caught the lower portion of her lungs, revealing nodules that looked like fungal pneumonia.

The surgeons immediately ordered a bronchoscopy to withdraw fluid for culture. The timing was a miracle; an hour later, Karis couldn't have tolerated that procedure. Instead of growing fungus, though, the cultures from her lungs were growing *bacteria*.

They had been giving Karis the wrong antibiotics.

An infectologist, who had done his PhD research on Legionella, rotated between several hospitals. This man, likely the only person in Pittsburgh capable of recognizing this early the specific bacteria growing in Karis's cultures, "happened" to be on duty at our hospital Friday morning. Yes. It was Legionella. There had not been a case of Legionnaire's Disease at this hospital in twelve years.

"So," Dr. M said, "each hour Karis stays alive strengthens our tiny flicker of hope a tiny bit—our tiny hope that there will be time for the correct antibiotics to fight the Legionella."

Why did he keep emphasizing the word "tiny"? Hope was hope. My heart grabbed it and held it tight.

Dr. M then explained a second huge challenge. Because they had stopped all immunosuppressant medication to treat her pneumonia, Karis's transplanted intestine was disintegrating. It had to be removed before Karis went into septic shock.

And her kidneys and liver were failing.

And Karis still required the oscillator.

And operating on a shaking body is impossible.

32

Karis had to stay alive long enough for the correct antibiotics — being life-flighted from the CDC to our hospital as we spoke — to combat the Legionella so she could transfer to a normal ventilator before she died from sepsis. Dr. M guessed she had at most two or three days to achieve this "magic window" for an attempted surgery.

I clung to the tiny flicker of hope: *Karis was still alive.*

In São Paulo, Brazil, meanwhile, as Valerie described it to me later: "I was at school running laps in P.E. Friday afternoon when Dad walked onto the field. He grabbed my arm and said, 'Get your things.' He acted weird and didn't speak all the way home. Then he told me to pack a suitcase for myself and one for him; he was too upset to do it himself. While we drove to the airport, he finally told me what was going on. We didn't know whether Karis would still be alive when we landed in Newark after our ten-hour flight. That was the worst trip I've ever made."

Karis *was* still alive when they touched down in Newark. The last leg of their trip was less fraught than the long flight from São Paulo.

Saturday afternoon, an ICU doctor told us he thought Karis had a chance of surviving.

Hour by hour, we kept vigil. Hour by hour word came that Karis still breathed. But getting her off the oscillator just wasn't happening. On 100 percent oxygen, her blood gases gradually began to improve, but altering her position even a little resulted in immediate decompensation. Every system of her body suffered from the double impact of virulent pneumonia and runaway rejection. As her kidneys and liver failed, our tiny flame of hope flickered.

Two days passed, then three — the outer limit the surgeons had postulated for attempting to remove Karis's disintegrating intestine. This surgery would be more difficult than the original transplant, and they would have to perform it as quickly as possible to limit her time under anesthesia.

Finally, Tuesday evening, Karis successfully transferred from the oscillator to an ordinary ventilator. At 7:45 the next morning, our family lined up in the hallway connecting the ICU to the surgical suite. Suddenly, the ICU double doors popped open. The surgical team came racing with Karis down the hallway to the OR. One doctor knelt precariously on her bed, pumping oxygen into her lungs as they ran. We yelled, "We love you, Karis!" and they disappeared.

And then it was waiting time again. We simply moved from the ICU waiting room down the hall and around the corner to the surgery waiting room.

Karis's doctors had given us no hope that she could survive such an invasive surgery. Her lungs, kidneys, liver, and intestine were all in terrible shape and her immune system was severely compromised. As the minutes ticked by, though, our optimism increased, and seven hours later, we lined up in the hallway again as they rushed Karis back to the ventilator in the ICU.

Against all odds, *she was still alive*. We breathed deeply of hope.

Karis herself, deeply sedated, missed the miracles that preserved her life. For seventy-four days in the ICU, most of that time in an induced coma, she and her physicians and hundreds of loving prayer warriors battled one setback after another.

One by one, she was released from the coma, from the ventilator, and—hallelujah!—from intensive care. A critical care physician told us Karis was the sickest patient ever to leave that ICU alive.

Her reaction?

"Mom, why did you worry? Of course, I didn't die. God still has plans for me here!"

Debra Kornfield framed her memoir *Karis: All I See Is Grace*, around her daughter's journals and poetry, then wrote a historical fiction trilogy. After twenty years in Brazil, Debra and her husband, David, adventure with their children and four grandchildren in Pittsburgh. Follow her on HorseThief1898.blog and devotionally on ButGod.blog.

Maswa's Story of God's Provision

Christie American Horse

The Ugandan sun peaks through the trees, shining into the window and brightening my heart as I begin my day. I walk through the four-room house, passing bedrooms bursting with beautiful children in their beds, and walk out the door. Hope fills my heart as I lift a prayer to my Redeemer.

My stomach grumbles, and I know how my children feel. The previous day, we had gone without food. I do not want to think about them going hungry, but my stomach pushes me there. The day's needs weigh heavily on me as I size them up. I know God will come through! I wonder how He will provide for them today. I force my focus on all that God has done throughout my life.

Gathering our water jugs together, I call the older children in charge of hauling water today. We begin the two-mile walk to dip water. We bring it back to be strained and boiled for drinking, cooking, and bathing. It is only the beginning of all the chores to do today.

I lead the children in prayer. We especially ask for our daily bread—for God to provide it today. I pray so hard and expect God to move. I know He will. I have no energy for doubt!

When we arrive back at the orphanage, my phone lights up. The message is from a brother in the Lord in the United States. He and another have wired money. I quickly make plans to go into town.

"Brother Alex, may I have a ride into town? I can pay for the gas once we get there."

"Sure," he replies. "I can come now so that we can return sooner." He knows that the children did not eat the previous day. When we return, I can help cook for the children," he adds. What a wonderful friend God has provided to us.

We travel forty miles on rough, dusty roads before we reach the city. We pass bicycles and motorcycles loaded with goods and produce for the markets.

As we travel, I see a child picking through a garbage pile and quickly eating what she finds. I feel the all-too-familiar hunger pangs begin knocking. I know that child feels even more hungry than I do, as she anxiously fumbles through the trash, hoping mercy will find her in the form of some food.

I close my eyes and envision a little boy picking through the well-known garbage heap, eating anything he can find. The small, beautiful boy cries to himself as he thinks, "I cannot stand this starvation!" As bad as the physical emptiness is that he feels in the pit of his stomach is, the more profound is the sadness that sinks his young spirit.

I see into the boy's past. His mother died when he was only a year old, and his father followed the next year. His dear, precious grandmother did the best she could. Pushing past her grief, she rented a small house and managed to care for her grandson for five more years until she succumbed to illness and passed on. I see this young child waiting in the house his grandmother had made into a home.

The boy hears a woman call at the doorway, and at that moment, he thinks, perhaps it might be his grandmother returning, but it is the owner of the little house. She looks into his sad eyes. His tear-stained face tells the story, but she has no time to read it. The house has been rented, and the child has to leave.

The story of Jesus and his love for children interrupts my thoughts. "Then people brought little children to Jesus for him to place his hands on them and pray for them. But the disciples rebuked them. Jesus said, Let the little children come to me, and do not hinder them, for the kingdom of heaven belongs to such as these." When he had placed his hands on them, he went on from there" (Matthew 19:13-14). But this little boy did not know what Jesus was planning for him.

As we near the town, Alex asks, "Are you alright, Maswa?"

"I was thinking about the children," I respond.

"Maswa," Alex says, "Your responsibility is great, with forty-five children in your care." A look of deep concern spreads across his face.

"Brother Alex, the responsibility is God's," I affirm. "He is Jehovah Jireh: the God who provides!" My enthusiasm for the God who has provided for us so many times in our gravest of moments flows out in other words of thankfulness as we pull up to the shop where we will receive funds from our dear partners worldwide. Today, these partners sent funds from the United States. One has sent one hundred dollars, and the other five hundred dollars, for a miraculous total of six hundred dollars!

These are enough funds to feed these innocent souls for ten days! "Praise God, brother Alex, for His boundless provision!" I blurt out.

Alex laughs with me as we cheerfully enter the shop. "Brother Maswa," Alex says with a smile. "Let me buy you some lunch. I worked yesterday," he continued. "You can feed me dinner."

"I will fast until my children eat," I replied with great thankfulness to God. "That will be soon enough."

I feel like a child in a candy shop as we walk through the markets, carefully selecting the food that will last the longest and provide the most nutrition for our kids. One woman always gives us a discount for the children, so we stop there. There is much to load, but we do it joyfully, thinking of the children with rumbling bellies breaking out in smiles at the plates of food they will soon have.

We thread through the traffic of buses, bicycles, children, and others loaded with the day's work. Soon, we hit a dirt road and the Ugandan countryside. The beauty of the season only adds to my enthusiasm.

On one side of the road, I see a brickyard. As we pass, I once again imagine the beautiful boy, now grown into a young man. He slaps the clay he has prepared into the molds, lining them up to harden, bake, and become bricks. *I had always dreamt of owning my own land to build a large home on, but, for now, I reside in a one-room house,* the young man thinks. The work is difficult in the hot sun, but his heart rejoices, thankful for it. He had saved enough to rent the land he saw the evening before. It was three miles from the village and forty miles out of town. From there, it was only two miles to dip drinking water in.

The man prays as he lays the bricks. "God, my Provider, help me afford this land."

We journey nearer to the village. Soon we will be cooking. Alex and I discuss the orphanage children, who desperately need our love and care. We provide a school, food, clothing, and medical care. It is weighty on my shoulders, but God always comes through.

Passing the village, I see three men building a house. The young man reappears in my mind. Two men are with him. Not only has he saved money for the land, but he has some left over to purchase enough timber and hire these men to help him cut it and build a four-room log home. It is basic but big enough to shelter the ever-increasing number of children continuing to ask him for help. Later, he plans to build a brick structure, perhaps to house, a school, or a church.

He has been feeling a call to preach the good news of Jesus Christ. He met God through a man from the orphanage who frequented the garbage pile to see which children needed his help most. One day, he took the beautiful little boy to the dorm. The orphanage workers fed him, and he received an education and the knowledge he would need to survive independently.

I commented, "Brother Alex, I see myself in the people in the streets today and know that God has used the suffering in my life as an orphan to strengthen and inspire me to build this orphanage."

He agrees as we pull into the orphanage land. Tiny feet run swiftly to greet us. The children know what it means when we go into the city. The older teenagers begin unloading the truck. They smile as they deliver the bags to the storage location. I am pleased that they are so thoughtful and helpful without being told.

The stronger children open bags. Other children help cook. The youngest lay out utensils and fill pots with hearty food. Children's laughter fills the air as they gleefully play, waiting for their little tummies to be nourished. Life is good! Indeed, God is El Jireh, the God who provides.

Christie American Horse is an ordained Elder in the Church of the Nazarene, with doctoral studies in evangelism and church planting. She is an educator with experience in cross-cultural ministry, church planting, restart ministry, as well as being an author, and artist. (Learn more about her at Amazon.com: Rev. Christie A. American Horse: books, biography, latest update. She met Maswa while serving in Uganda.

Seeing God's Provision

Chris T. Wells

"Jehovah Jireh, my Provider . . ." Humming this favorite tune, I opened my Bible, but a little voice piped up from across the room before I could select a chapter.

"Mommy, my tummy hurts."

My nine-year-old daughter cradled her stomach as she approached me.

"Again?"

A frown creased her little face. "Yes. I wish it would stop hurting." She sighed, causing my own stomach to twist into a knot.

"Me, too, baby. Let me get you something. Sit here; I'll be right back."

Laying my book aside, I rose and headed to the bathroom, as my brain began to churn, trying once again to decipher what could be causing the pain. Stopping in front of the medicine cabinet, I stared blindly into the mirror for a moment, reviewing the facts.

Macayle's stomach aches had been increasing over the past year. There was no discernible pattern, although I had certainly looked for one. She'd been allergy tested for wheat, corn, gluten, nuts, dairy, lactose, and more. Nothing. Dust? Not it. Cat fur? No. Muscle sprain from the strange gymnastic moves girls like to do? Nope. The stomachaches were random, and they were not intestinally related.

Regular over-the-counter medicines didn't touch the pain. My mother, who had earned the title of "health-food nut" way back in the 1970s, had provided many holistic remedies, to no avail. I had done everything the doctor recommended, and she was out of ideas. Every known cure this side of acupuncture had been given a shot to stop the pain, with no results.

I opened the medicine cabinet and reached for a dark blue bottle. A few months earlier, while scouring the health food store, I had found a strange homeopathic tincture that had brought a tiny amount of relief to my daughter. I walked back to the living room, putting on my "Everything's going to be alright" smile.

"Here you go, sweetie." I provided the dropper, which she liked to squeeze herself, and watched my beloved girl put the drops under her tongue, trying not to let my worry show.

She always knew.

"I'll be okay, Mom. Really."

I hugged her close. *She's no quitter. I'll give her that much.* She functioned through the stomachaches regularly, unless they came with a rare headache. I sat back down, and she put her head in my lap. As I rubbed her tummy gently, her eyes closed. Of course, individual aches and pains were dealt with as they cropped up, but this was starting to spiral out of control.

My mind raced with unanswered questions. I felt tears beginning to form and looked away. The Bible still lay open nearby. The pages had flipped, and the underlined words of Philippians 4:19 jumped out at me. "And my God shall supply all your need according to His riches in glory by Christ Jesus."

I blinked. *Why haven't I asked for help sooner?*

Feeling a glimmer of hope, I turned to Jesus, my longtime Savior, Ever-Present Help, and Confidante. "Jesus, please heal Macayle. I need You to do it. Thank you that Your strength is made perfect in my weakness, because I am too weak to help Your precious daughter. I've tried everything, but now I'm putting her into Your hands, Father. In Jesus' name I pray and trust, amen."

I took a deep breath and looked around, but no miracle cure borne on angel wings appeared. However, a sense of peace that I couldn't explain settled in my heart and mind and quieted my worries.

Macayle put her little hand over mine on her tummy and said, "Amen."

About a week later, Macayle's third-grade teacher contacted me. Mr. C had previously taught my oldest son.

"Mrs. Wells, I'm concerned. Macayle is super smart but can't do math like I'd expect from one of your kids. She struggles with the problems. Perhaps you should have her eyes checked."

Macayle had never once complained about her eyes, but I respected this teacher and readily agreed.

Soon afterward, I sat in the darkened room of the family eye doctor as he ran some tests.

"Nothing is wrong with her sight," Dr. J concluded. "She has 20/20 vision."

Baffled, I pressed him. "Why would her teacher think she has eye trouble then?"

He meditated on the huge ophthalmoscope filling the tiny examining room for a long moment before abruptly excusing himself with a, "Just a moment, please."

Frustrated, I grabbed Macayle's hand and prayed. "Oh Jesus, please provide us the help we need." I tried not to bite my lip as my girl looked at me.

"Amen," she said softly.

A few minutes later, Dr. J returned with another doctor in tow. "I'd like you to meet my colleague, Juanita Collier. She's a behavioral optometrist with a specialty in vision therapy. I've asked her to take a look at Macayle."

Dr. Collier was young, just starting out in her practice. Although she had a serious demeanor, she greeted us pleasantly.

"Hello Macayle; I hear you're having trouble with your math problems. Is that right?"

Macayle nodded.

"Well, let's take a look. I'd like you to follow this wand with your eyes, please."

Out of her doctor's coat, she pulled a fifteen–inch wand with a small gold ball at the tip. She moved the wand left to right and up and down, like the sign of the cross, then made a wide circle. After a mere ten seconds of motion, she stopped and turned to me.

"Macayle's eyes don't track together, causing stress and strain as the left and right eye muscles fight against each other. That's why, even though she has perfect vision, her eyes are not working together to see the math problems between the board and her paper. Make an appointment with me for vision therapy. We can fix this."

I was dumbfounded. She sounded so confident. Could it be as simple as she said? A question popped up in my mind. "Would a condition like this possibly cause stomachaches?"

"Absolutely," the good doctor replied matter-of-factly. "Our entire body system is connected. When muscles don't work in sync like they should, they transmit the tension and strain to other body parts. The stomach muscle is definitely impacted. I see that commonly."

"It never would have occurred to me," I said in wonder.

Dr. Collier nodded. "I know, right? There are many children and adults who have unexplainable aches and pains, coordination troubles, clumsiness, and even motion sickness that no one suspects are vision related."

While still a bit shocked, I felt compelled to take immediate action. "Thank you so much! I'll set up an appointment right away."

"Let me give you my card because I'm moving to my own practice in another town next week."

"Next week?" I paused as my heart skipped a beat at the closeness of the timing. "Oh, my goodness. Well, wherever your new office is, we will be there."

Dr. Collier nodded and turned to Macayle. "Then, we'll see you soon. And we'll make those math troubles, stomachaches, and anything else go away for good."

"Okay!" Macayle agreed eagerly.

When both doctors had gone from the examining room Macayle looked at me. "I guess Jesus heard our prayer, Mom."

"He always does, sweetie. But yes, that was fast!" A giggle escaped since I was still in a bit of a daze. Taking a moment, I thanked God for His perfect timing and amazing grace in causing us to cross paths with a type of doctor I never even knew existed.

What followed were many months of driving to weekly vision therapy appointments. I watched in awe as the exceptional Dr. Collier and her team used eye exercises designed to strengthen and correct Macayle's specific vision problem without medicine or surgery. The dark blue bottle grew dusty in the cabinet as we continued the exercises at home, and her unexplainable stomachaches disappeared completely.

Nine years later, I held my breath as Macayle opened the response from her first-choice engineering college. My eyes conjured up that little girl and remembered how our beautiful Jesus had provided at just the right time — to move her from a place of unexplained, debilitating pain to being a confident, healthy young woman. But the prayer of thanks forming on my lips was interrupted.

"Look Mom! It says, 'We are pleased to accept Macayle Wells into our program as a mathematics major.' Yay!"

She jumped up and hugged me, and I pulled her close. With her soft hair next to my face, I looked upward and said, "Thank you, Jesus."

Macayle laughed and pulled back, waving the letter in the air. "Amen!"

When Chris T. Wells received a strong impression from God to start writing stories about His provision, fifteen minutes a day was all she could squeeze from everyday life. Yet, God seemed to say, "That is plenty." The results? New path, new friends, new tales to tell. Visit BackstoriesOfTheBible.com.

Salvaged by Hope

Michelle Marie

Alone in the driver's seat, I stared across a vast, empty parking lot. My teary gaze was fixed on a light pole at the other end, rising high above a solid cement base. Was the distance great enough? Could I reach a speed sufficient to put an end to my rock bottom?

I was alone in a city five hours from home, where work contacts were the only people I knew. My job had always been my refuge. No matter how poorly I lived up to expectations in other aspects of my life, I could always prove myself worthy through career success.

But on this day, failure haunted me there as well. The façade had cracked. I'd become so overwhelmed by the noise in my head that I'd walked out on the person I held in the highest regard—my boss. She had been my go-to through some tough times over the past few years. She was the last person I knew who valued me and the least deserving of my meltdown. Indeed, she would know I just needed to clear my head and that this was out of character.

Once I regained control of my emotions, the opportunity to explain didn't happen. She was livid and left town. I was devastated. On top of all else, I'd pushed her too far, and she had also given up on me.

To most people, my life looked as calm and beautiful as the ocean on a sunny day. I was always on the go, planned annual beach vacations with friends, actively participated in ski club travel and day trips, played golf as often as retired folk, and still managed to be an overachiever at work.

Most didn't realize that every ounce of energy I had, and more was going into trying to maintain that perfect life. They were unaware of the chaos behind the scenes. So much was weighing me down that I was constantly fighting to keep my head above water. I was burnt out, exhausted, and drowning.

Even though the sea may appear calm on the surface, a massive storm can be brewing underneath. Just like the ocean waves, there are highs and lows in life. Sometimes, we feel like we're in control, treading water. At other times, we lose our grasp and go under. Similar to currents that produce slight fluctuations in the water level but cause a treacherous undertow hidden entirely beneath the surface. These are difficult to detect from shore but so dangerous to someone in the thick of it.

I was kicking frantically to keep my head afloat, but with even the slightest shift of what was on my shoulders, I swallowed more water. I was sinking. I was in crisis. The most profound feeling of hopelessness washed over me. Couldn't anyone see through the illusion of calm on the surface? Didn't they know the depth of my despair? Why did I feel so alone?

Something drew my attention back to my quirky little rescue dog. As cute as she was, there was something under the surface that no one understood, and I'd been her last hope, too. I couldn't abandon her in that hotel room, far from home and anyone else she knew. Back, I went for the night, and the next day, I drove home.

I called to make amends with my boss. She recommended counseling. I couldn't imagine taking that step, but my apology would be hollow if I denied help. She provided contact information for three counselors. I choose one who was a Christian therapist, even though I hadn't attended church in 35 years.

I wrote an inquiry to this counselor several times before I actually sent it. Indeed, I'd challenge the "never too messy, too broken, or too far gone for God" theory she posted in her information. I was positive lightning would strike if I entered a church, but it was probably not wise to admit that upfront. It was likely best to sleep on it and reconsider this email in the morning. I'd saved the draft, and . . . hit send by mistake!

But God knew precisely what he was doing! God knew my resolve to be strong and independent. He knew why I'd chosen to swim alone for so long. I'd tugged on His lifeline without even recognizing Who secured it many times. He counted every tear and carried me through times I didn't realize.

Looking back, it's clear that I'd been buoyed up by His love and strength for much longer than I acknowledged. Oh, how He must have cringed at the lessons that hurt me and delighted in those that left me relatively unscathed. And He knew I needed to be pulled right out of the water and salvaged from the rocks at the bottom. As God the Provider, He needed to restore my hope. He took this cue and enacted His rescue plan in a way that only God can!

Fifteen minutes into the next workday, I received a response from this counselor. She was not taking new clients. However, something told her that she needed to get me in, so she would make a concession. She had a cancellation for the next day.

Seriously? Tomorrow? Within the twenty-four-hour cancellation period. No backing out once I said yes. The time between my yes and my arrival at her office was a bit of a blur. I was nervous, mainly about the Jesus thing. I had doubts about even going. *I could handle this. I'd survived worse before.* The previous week had just been a moment in time. Sure, I was having difficulty quieting the noise in my head and controlling my emotions since my brother's passing two months earlier, but that would get better soon. I'd gotten through the grief of losing Dad a few years ago in just a few months.

There'd been much focus on mental illness since the pandemic, but I made it through ok. I was too tough and independent to be unwell. I was sure I'd look like a fool for wasting her time. It's not like there was anything in my life I couldn't fix on my own, but I'd go through the motions to appease.

As I rode the elevator up to her office, my mind continued to churn. I was convinced this visit was pointless. I avoided showing others my emotions at all costs. I found it difficult to verbalize my thoughts. No one ever understood me. That in itself was highly frustrating and frequently resulted in tears. If I couldn't open up to people I knew, it was hopeless to think I'd open up to a stranger. Did I need to make a fool of myself, too? She'd made a concession, so I couldn't just leave.

The office door opened, and I was invited in. I took a deep breath and followed her lead. She made our time together relatively easy. She asked questions that probed at some wounds but didn't open any. As I gained the courage to raise my gaze from the floor, I noticed the tattoo on her forearm. The very thing I needed most: HOPE!

"May the God of hope fill you with all joy and peace in believing, so that by the power of the Holy Spirit you may abound in hope" (Romans 15:13 ESV).

I didn't know why, but something told me this was where I needed to be. Despite my fear of opening old wounds, I agreed to return.

That single act of courage has changed everything. It was not overnight and not even noticeable to me for a while. True to the counselor's word, she never raised faith as a topic never spoke of God and never preached. She never promised God wouldn't pursue me, though, and He has done so relentlessly! He has shown up everywhere, in everything, and continually orchestrates the most incredible coincidences that only God could engineer. He led me to a church where I not only felt welcomed but also felt wanted.

He's blessed me with a loving community and new friendships that raise me, and He's the best listener I've ever known.

God brought me through the eye of the storm and raised me up from the murky water. He's opened my eyes to the inner peace He provides when we are in a relationship with Him. It's much easier to keep my head above water when floating and trusting Him to maintain the calm beneath the surface. He's shown me that those who've weathered such storms are the best teachers to lead others by example and show them what God can do. All He asks is that we trust in Him. My hope is in God, and my soul is firmly anchored in His faithfulness and provision.

Michelle Marie is a new Christian and new writer. The therapist in whom she found hope and the pastor who's nurtured her faith story — her bookends—have inspired her to share His grace. She writes the stories that she needed to hear on her journey to the brink and back.

When We Feel Abandoned

April M. Whitt

As I look back on the past few years and my struggle with cancer, I have often felt discouraged. It first began in January 2020 when I was diagnosed with colon cancer, and my journey continues today with setbacks as well as victories, but I am still here and doing pretty well!

Initially, I had surgery and chemotherapy. Those days went by in something of a blur because I was probably in shock and hardly believed what was happening to me. But when I finished the chemo, I thought I would be cancer-free. However, two years later (in 2022), the cancer returned. This time, it was not in my organs (Thank You, Lord!) but in my abdomen, near my colon, below my liver.

Naturally, the second diagnosis felt devastating. Thoughts of eternity consumed me as I prepared for what might be the end of my days. I was a believer, but this serious condition challenged my faith. It was easy to fall into thinking that God had abandoned me.

Then, one day, as I sat on my couch crying and feeling sorry for myself, I heard from God. His voice wasn't exactly audible, yet He yelled at me! He "shouted" into my right ear and said: "I will *never* leave you or forsake you!" I straightened up some after that. And, He has continued to lead me over mountain tops and through valleys of the shadow with His presence nearby.

I have learned (and am still learning) to trust Him. I need to allow Him to lead me where I should go. And when I look at Exodus 14:5–28, the scripture helps me to see that

God has me where He wants me. I'm reminded that if He has allowed troubles into my life, it must be for His greater purpose. And though I may feel trapped by the Egyptian army and pressed against The Red Sea, I am exactly where He wants me to be. I'm finding comfort in that reality, and learning to relax and let go, while I wait for Him to open a way

God doesn't owe me any more days on this earth, and He already gave me His best when He gave me eternal life through Christ. It's just hard not to be greedy for more. I must remember that He is in control and truly has good things for me.

Mary and Martha thought Jesus had abandoned them, too. When their brother Lazarus died, Jesus waited four days before He showed up to help them. Those four days were probably very long. I know my mind can go a lot of places in a short time, and I'm sure they became discouraged.

Even though Mary and Martha knew Jesus in ways that most of us have not, they still allowed themselves to fear. They'd seen His physical presence, experienced His miracles, and even regarded Him as a friend. But when He stayed away at their time of great need, they may have begun to think He didn't care.

In John 11:35, the Bible says that when Jesus finally met up with Mary and the others, He wept. But I don't think He was grieved over losing His friend because He knew that He had power over life and death. I believe, instead, He was moved out of compassion for his hurting friends. I think He cared so much that He felt their sorrow as if it were His own.

God is not unkind, even though He can be hard on us. He tests our faith to reveal the greater truth that He is our Savior. And Mary and Martha knew Him as Savior as well. We know this because they believed that Lazarus would rise on the last day. But even with the hope of eternity, they wanted their prayers answered now, just like we do. And like us, they probably began to experience doubt.

Doubt is a human emotion not easily defeated. The good news is that God is a forgiving God, and His blood covers all. But we must trust Him to live in contentment without much stress and fear. Even when we don't know the outcome or if the hopes and dreams we've worked for will ever come to pass, we need to trust that He really does have the best plan.

So, as I wait beside the Red Sea, I rest in His grace. Even when things seem as dead and hopeless as a four-day-old body in a grave, I can recall what Jesus told Martha:

"I Am The Resurrection and the life!" He said. And with this, we cannot fail. Our hope is secure in Him because He will never leave or forsake us!

April M. Whitt is a Christian blogger, children's book author, and illustrator. She is a retired school teacher who is enjoying life with her husband in their empty nest, visiting their grandchildren, continuing to survive cancer, and looking forward to what God is going to do next!

A Mother's Desperate Prayer

Mary Dodge Allen

I sat in the darkened room in Parkland Hospital's burn unit and listened in anguish as my four-year old son whimpered in pain, while morphine dripped through his IV. Tormented by guilt, my mind replayed vivid images of those harrowing moments three days earlier, when my carelessness had caused his agonizing burns.

At dinnertime Davey had been sitting on his booster seat at the kitchen table. He had just been bathed and was dressed in lightweight pajamas. I was in a hurry as I lifted a casserole dish from the oven, and I didn't realize cheese sauce had bubbled over. My thick oven mitts made it hard to keep a firm grip on the slippery handles. The glass dish fell against the edge of the table and broke apart. Steaming food splattered everywhere.

Davey screamed.

My husband scooped Davey out of his booster seat and rushed him to the sink. He unbuttoned Davey's pajama top and ran a gentle stream of cool water over his chest and left arm to rinse off the scalding food. I watched, horrified, as Davey's burned skin slid away from his body. We bundled him in clean towels and drove to the community hospital close to our home. My body shook uncontrollably as I sat in the car, rocking Davey in my arms. *What have I done to our only child, our precious son? Will he survive?*

The burns on Davey's chest, left arm, and thigh were so severe, the ER staff decided to transfer him Parkland Hospital's burn unit, thirty miles away. I rode in the ambulance with Davey. My husband followed in our car, but he wasn't allowed to enter Parkland's overcrowded, standing-room-only emergency room.

For several hours, I stood next to Davey's ambulance cot in a dazed shock. Fear and dread sat like lead weights in my stomach. I found it hard to breathe, as if I were struggling to stay afloat in a stormy, chaotic sea of shouting, wailing, hurting people. I murmured soothing words of comfort to my son as I stroked his baby-fine hair. The Snoopy balloon my husband had tied to his ambulance cot twirled and bobbed as people brushed past us. Davey's eyes followed the balloon's constant movement, and he occasionally smiled.

A familiar face appeared in the crowd. I felt a surge of relief when our pastor joined us. After he prayed with me, he described a surprisingly similar burn trauma in his own family. When his youngest brother had been Davey's age, he had scalded his chest and arms by pulling a pan of boiling water off the stove. His brother's burns eventually healed, but his mother put herself through a needless amount of suffering by blaming herself for the accident. Our pastor truly empathized with me, but I was too distraught to be comforted.

Davey was finally admitted to Parkland's burn unit. My husband rejoined us, accompanied by a social worker. I knew all about child abuse investigations, since I had worked as a social worker before my marriage. As she questioned me, I stood with my head bowed and responded in a monotone, feeling totally unfit to be any child's mother.

Then she asked Davey to tell her what happened.

"Mommy dropped the dish." He turned his wide, blue-eyed gaze on me. "Why did you do that, Mommy?"

I could no longer choke back my tears.

My husband wrapped his arm around my shoulders. "It was an accident, Davey. Mommy didn't mean to drop it."

My legs weakened. I sank into the chair by Davey's bed and covered my face with my hands as I sobbed.

"Don't cry, Mommy. It was an accident."

I wept even harder. My precious son was trying to comfort me, after all the pain I had caused him. When my tears were finally spent, I looked up. The social worker was gone.

For the next three days, I stayed by Davey's side. He was placed on antibiotics because infection — always a danger in severe burns — is especially life-threatening to small children. Twice every day, nurses carefully washed his burns with antibiotic soap. Since even the lightest touch to his burned skin produced excruciating pain, these baths were sheer torture for Davey. His shrill cries tore right through me. I would have gladly traded places to spare him this agony. But I could do nothing. I couldn't even pray. I felt horribly ashamed, distanced from God.

On that third night at Parkland hospital, as I listened to my son's soft whimpering, I seriously considered suicide. I could no longer cope with seeing Davey in such intense pain; a pain I had caused. And I knew I couldn't bear to live if he died.

In desperation, I whispered my first prayer. "Lord, please forgive me. Help me."

Immediately, I felt as if I were being lifted up by a soft breeze. My body seemed to be floating, suspended in the room. An indescribable feeling of love wrapped around me like a soft, warm blanket. And then a voice flowed through me; a gentle voice with a tone of authority, saying:

You are forgiven. Be strong for Davey. He needs you now, more than ever. I am with you. I will never leave you. Trust Me.

As the comforting warmth surrounded me, I felt calm . . . secure . . . like a baby resting in loving arms. Then slowly and tenderly, the arms released me.

I heard Davey's soft whimpering in the darkened room. Outside the closed door, I heard the echo of quick footsteps and the muffled voices of nurses as they passed. Somewhere down the hallway, a burn patient cried out and then another moaned. Nothing had changed. Except me.

Instead of being tortured by remorse, I felt an inexplicable peace. Hope had replaced despair. My focus had suddenly shifted from how I had failed Davey, to how I could help him through this. I had no idea what the future held, but I would do whatever I could for my son and trust God with the outcome.

The following day, Davey's physician told us that the second-degree burns on his chest and left arm would eventually heal with proper care, but the third-degree burn on his thigh might need a skin graft. During the last week of his stay in the burn unit, the nurses taught me how to give Davey sterile baths and then bandage his wounds. I wanted him to come home more than anything, but I dreaded the prospect of giving him those painful baths twice a day. Worry began overshadowing the peace that had lingered deep inside me.

His first bath at home was a nightmare. My husband knelt next to me at the side of the bathtub and struggled to hold Davey still while I bathed him. Whenever I gently touched Davey's raw burned skin with the soft, sterile gauze cloth, he flinched and screamed, "Stop Mommy, stop! It hurts!"

I broke into a cold sweat. *Why is God punishing me like this? Haven't I caused my son enough suffering?* As Davey continued squirming and crying, I prayed for the strength to continue bathing him. I asked God to guide my hands, to help me wash the burns thoroughly enough to remove germs, yet gently enough to leave the new, healing skin intact. Somehow, we finished Davey's bath that evening. After we re-bandaged his burns, we settled him into bed.

I was still trembling, and my husband looked pale when we walked into the kitchen. My mother, who had come from out of state to help, poured fresh coffee for us. I sat down at the table and reached for my mug. Then I froze. It was the coffee mug my husband had given me on Mother's Day, decorated with hearts and the phrase: WORLD'S GREATEST MOM. I pushed it away, feeling too exhausted to cry.

The dreaded, painful baths continued twice a day, for four long months. But as I witnessed Davey's gradual healing—the growth of pink, healthy skin beneath the raw, burned area—I began to view his burn care in a new light. It wasn't my punishment. It was the path for me to help Davey to get well. His burns, caused by my carelessness, eventually healed under my care. And a skin graft wasn't needed.

Our son is now married. His skin has healed well, with only a few visible burn scars, and his memory of the experience has receded. But I clearly remember, with gratitude, God's merciful answer to my desperate prayer. His supernatural, loving presence filled me with a peace beyond understanding and helped me to turn away from despair and self-blame. Each time I focused on trusting God, I felt His faithful presence, giving me the strength I needed to handle the challenging job of Davey's burn care. And what I cherish most is how, as He enabled my hands to cleanse and heal my son's physical wounds, His divine grace was at work, healing my emotional wounds.

Philippians 4:6–7: *Do not be anxious about anything, but in every situation, by prayer and petition, with thanksgiving, present your requests to God. And the peace of God, which transcends all understanding, will guard your hearts and your minds in Christ Jesus.*

Mary Dodge Allen, award-winning author, lives in Florida. She's won: Christian Indie Award; Angel Award; multiple Royal Palm Literary Awards. She's also a blogger at *Heroes, Heroines and History*, www.hhhistory.com. Website: www.marydodgeallen.com.

Storms of Our Lives

Sally Gano Jones

Our lives were falling apart. How could so many things go wrong all at once? It wasn't just one little thing. No matter which way we turned, something was going wrong.

As Christians, my husband and I both trusted in the Lord. He had always cared for us through stormy periods and been our provider. However, this walk through the valley seemed longer and more troubling during this season of our lives. *How would God provide for our many needs?*

My husband's company of the previous twelve years talked about "downsizing" and "reduction in force." David and his fellow managers were on pins and needles, wondering, "Who's next?" Some were jumping ship before the dreaded news came. Trusting that doing your job well and working hard could provide any sense of job security was hard to do at that time.

There was also a "Will Contest" because a family tried to take all of the acreage from the family farm from David. It was expensive to hire lawyers to defend what he believed was his inheritance, but we had no other recourse.

Our daughter's marriage was crumbling, too. She needed our support as she faced an uncertain future while raising two small boys. We were trying to be there for her and our grandsons. Times were difficult.

My aging mother's health was fine, and then, suddenly, she began to have falls. I traveled to spend time with her and help her get stabilized. She was ninety-five.

We prayed. We talked to God. We attended a Christian retreat in North Carolina, and a kind chaplain prayed with us. The guest speaker at the conference spoke on Matthew 8: 23–27 that weekend: The disciples were in a furious storm in a boat with Jesus. Jesus calmly slept through the storm. His anxious disciples awakened Him, crying, "Lord, save us! We're going to drown!" (Matthew 8:25, NIV)

We identified with those anxious disciples. We, too, felt like we were drowning in our troubles in the middle of a raging storm at sea.

Lord, do you care about our troubles? I pondered these thoughts as I listened to the message. Yet, I also felt hope. God had provided for me so many times throughout my life. He was faithful. I know *He hears my prayers.*

I had retired from my teaching job several years before this. As I prayed through all these rumors of downsizing and possible job cuts in my husband's business, I decided I should update my teacher resume and look at some possible teaching positions again. So I did.

Meanwhile, the dreaded day finally came. My husband was asked to report to a meeting with an area manager in a town several hours away. He received the bad news that he would be released from his duties for a company "reduction in force." The timing was just a few weeks before David's sixtieth birthday. He was told to return to his local office that night to turn in his badge and keys. It was a very sad evening. I'd watched David work so hard for many years and give his best to his career. *How could they do this to him?*

We were praying daily about what to do with our lives. God was listening. El Jireh began to provide for us, but not in the way we expected. I received a phone call from a neighboring county school board. The lady on the phone was a personnel director for that school board.

"Is this Sally Jones?" she asked. I heard loud noises in the background.

"Yes," I replied, "but I'm having trouble hearing you!"

"Oh, that's because I'm on my lawnmower. I called because I saw your teaching resume online and would like to ask if you'd come into our county office for an interview?"

"Well, yes, of course!" I replied. I was shocked that someone responded to my resume so quickly.

She gave me an appointment time and an address for the interview. I went and listened to a very kind school principal. I answered his questions to the best of my ability. To our amazement, I was offered a job the next day, and I was to start teaching full-time again in three weeks.

When I shared this news, David looked relieved. He gave me a smile I'd not seen for weeks. Our Provider, El Jireh, was helping us make ends meet during this transition.

"This will give you time to look for another job," I assured him. We both realized the timing of this job offer was an answered prayer.

So, as the door at my husband's company closed tightly shut, another door opened for me to return to teaching full-time. We wouldn't have the same salary and benefits we'd been used to, but we would have enough income for groceries and other basic needs.

While I was teaching school, David diligently worked on job applications and participated in interviews that looked promising. We didn't have a solution to our long-term needs right away, but we were both trying very hard to continue to trust the Lord while working at what we knew would help us financially. We continued participating in our local church and small group and asked for prayer support from church staff and friends.

Several job opportunities did open for David's extensive engineering experience. Just when we thought the right door had opened for him, that door abruptly closed. It was confusing.

"Lord, we don't understand," we prayed. Meanwhile, we continued supporting our family members who needed us; our daughter and my mother, who lived out of state, needed physical and spiritual support. We put our worries in El Jireh's hands while we helped our family.

After several months of diligent job searching and interviews, David received a call from a recruiter. He was asked to interview in Ohio. We both preferred to stay in the southern U.S. but ran out of choices. The Ohio interview went very well, and then David was asked about working in Tulsa, Oklahoma, for this company. It would be further from family than we'd ever lived. We prayed and asked the Lord for guidance. We accepted the invitation to visit Tulsa and see the area for ourselves.

David accepted the Tulsa, Oklahoma, job. It was the only door that opened so wide. Our move was completely paid for. We found a house to lease within two days of searching. Then, miraculously, our Tennessee home sold within three days.

God had opened the door very wide for David's new job opportunity. El Jireh was providing for us in more ways than we could count.

Another surprise for God bringing us to Tulsa came when a medical diagnosis required me to have serious surgery: heart valve replacement. I had been too busy to figure out why my chest often ached and why I felt difficulty breathing. I asked my doctors, "Am I okay, because I don't feel okay?"

"No, you're not okay; we need to send you to the cardiologists at the main hospital," the kind doctor shared with me as he gave me four aspirin to swallow.

A few weeks after cardiologists ran several tests, I learned I had a serious congenital heart condition. I would need surgery to replace my aortic valve because it was "critical." The procedure I needed was available in Tulsa, and not readily available in other cities because it was still a relatively new procedure in the United States. The hospital assigned me to a "heart team," and some of the very best cardiothoracic surgeons supervised my care and treatment.

One of my doctors had previously done heart transplants, and I thought, *"If he can do heart transplants, I can trust him to repair my heart valve."*

El Jireh provides more than we even know how to ask. He provides and opens doors we need to walk through but closes doors we shouldn't go through. His divine wisdom guided us to Tulsa for David's job and also for my heart.

More prayers were answered during that difficult season. A judge overturned the invalid will concerning my husband's family farm, and David was deeded his farm property. Our daughter came through a very difficult time. My mother thrived and received excellent care. And then, because of the best heart healthcare in Tulsa, my new home, my heart works like new!

El Jireh walked with us through a difficult season. He met all our needs at the right time.

Sally Gano Jones is a Christian wife, mother and grandmother, as well as a retired school teacher, currently living near Tulsa, Oklahoma. She began writing at age eleven and later published her first piece, her testimony, *Decision* magazine, while she was studying English at the University of Florida.

And my God will supply every need of yours according

to his riches in glory in Christ Jesus.

— *Philippians 4:19, ESV*

Encouragement When We Need it Most

Sheila Boehning

I sorted through many outfits, not finding any that provided the confidence or look I wanted for a meeting with a new boss. I was nervous, feeling underqualified, overweight, and overall overwhelmed and intimidated. As I walked into a coffee shop that morning for a meeting preceding the meeting, a stranger said, "I saw you get out of your car and told my friend you look like a million bucks!"

God used a stranger to encourage. Those words provided confidence as I faced the meetings of the day, but more than that, they reminded me that God knows my thoughts and concerns and God, El Jireh, would provide all I needed for that job. He continually provides timely encouragement through words, notes, and actions.

In 1 Samuel 23, we read about a time in David's life when David was the God–chosen king of Israel, but Saul was the reigning king of Israel, who had made it his mission to kill David. David became a fugitive who was constantly on the run. He had no home, no earthly security, was continually at war, and was on guard for a king who wanted him dead. Ironically, David's best friend was the king's son, Jonathan. These best friends had made a pact to bless and care for each other and their families no matter what the future held.

David served King Saul by fighting and winning many battles, yet King Saul purposed to destroy David. Among Israel's ardent enemies were the Philistines. During a particular battle, David learned that the Philistines were attacking Keilah. He asked God what to do about the Philistines and if he should rescue the people of Keilah.

Amid all this running from Saul, David was still doing his job and fighting battles for Saul's kingdom. God said to attack and save Keilah, but when David led his men in the attack, they were afraid, even there in Judah. David's men were weak, and their faith in God was small. So, David asked God again. This task seemed so large. David knew his army's faith was so small. How would God provide?

This makes me think of an experience our family had. Our family loves to watch hockey, and we became avid Detroit Red Wing fans. That was back in the day when the Red Wings dominated hockey, winning the Stanley Cup in 1997, 1998, and 2002 with Shanahan, Yzerman, Lidstrom, Federov, Datsyuk, and, of course, the goalie, Dominik Hasek.

The year we lived in Budapest, Hungary, we decided to visit Czech Republic, home of my son, Graysen's, favorite player, the famous goalie Dominik Hasek. Graysen would spend hours watching Hasek play. He had several jerseys and posters of Hasek and even collected playing cards of Hasek. He had a goalie mask, stick, gloves, and pads, knew different moves, and desired nothing more than to be a goalie just like this outstanding Red Wing.

When we arrived in Prague, with its rows and rows of houses and historic cathedrals, he told us he wanted to visit Hasek's house. We told him we had no idea where Hasek lived. My very determined five-year-old looked at us puzzled and said that wasn't a problem—just start knocking on doors.

Oh, if only our faith to overcome obstacles were as uninhibited as a child's, if only we could so simplistically trust God to provide!

This Philistine army had a huge obstacle to overcome, but they had a huge God who had told them that they would overcome it. They could trust, El Jireh, to provide for them. They may have been a newly formed army and young in their faith, but their God assured David He would provide victory, and they would defeat the Philistines at Keilah.

David didn't fight any battle in his strength. He always battled in the power of El Jireh, the God who provides. David's men had a long way to go in trusting God to provide what He promised. They still needed to learn to trust Him to provide for them regardless of the tasks He placed before them.

David attacked, and God provided the victory. Shortly after this victory, Saul received word that David was in Keilah, so he planned to attack David because Saul's mission was still to destroy David. David asked God what to do next. He was concerned that Saul would pour out his wrath on the people of Keilah, as he had on the people of Nob, killing so many of them in his quest to annihilate David.

David feared that the people would turn him over to Saul, even though he had saved them the Philistines. God indeed told David to leave because Saul was coming, and that the people would betray him. So, he and all 600 of his men left. He trusted El Jireh to provide all that he needed. Again, David asked God what to do, and he followed God's directions. He didn't trust in his military expertise or try to do things in his way or his timing. He focused on the God who sees and knows everything and had the purpose for his life all mapped out. Complete of faith in His provider.

After leaving Keilah, David and his men journeyed into the strongholds. Every day, Saul hunted David, but God did not let him be seen (vs. 14). Can you imagine? Every single day, you are being hunted by your best friend's dad.

Jonathan visited David to help him find strength in God and to remind him of God's promises. What a risk Jonathan, the prince of Israel, took to seek out David, yet God provided encouragement, respite, and a best friend just when David needed it. Jonathan reminded David that his father would not be able to kill David because God had promised that he would be the king.

Jonathan could have visited David and rehashed all of the wrongs his dad had done, and they could have spent hours complaining and regurgitating each of Saul's faults, but they didn't. Instead, Jonathan pointed David to God's promises. He focused on God's ability to provide *all* that David needed. He got him refocused on seeing God, the El Jireh.

How often when a friend has been wronged, do we sit down with a cup of coffee iced tea and have a long gripe session? We do a play-by-play of each scenario when we were hurt, or our feathers were ruffled. What does that accomplish? It's pointless, exhausting, and emotionally draining! We should take a page from Jonathan and use that time and energy to refocus on God, realizing that He controls all parts of the story. He is El Jireh and will provide all we need, whether wisdom, forgiveness, guidance, encouragement, or strength. God will provide.

What a blessing it must have been to have Jonathan's encouragement because in Ziph men were scheming how they could help trap David and turn him over to Saul. After this encounter, David moved further into the wilderness in Maon for safety. Still, he moved refreshed and encouraged by his best friend, Jonathan, because through him, God, El Jireh, encouraged David to continue. This same God is fully aware of all we face and promises to provide for each one of us as well, at exactly the most pertinent time. He is El Jireh, and He will provide.

Sheila Boehning is passionate about encouraging others to rest in and trust the El Jireh who faithfully provides. She has been a teacher and administrator for elementary to graduate school level, nationally and internationally, for over 35 years. She delights in being a wife, mom, and Grammie.

The Second Coming

Bonnie Herrick

On a star-spangled night with a new moon on Maui, little Levi Lowe accompanied his father to the summit of Halealakalā for a viewing through the Pan-STARRS1 telescope. Young Levi was so proud to be the son of a prominent scientist that he hardly noticed the bitter cold or upset stomach that came with the elevation. He was anxious to help track the anomaly recently discovered by one of his father's colleagues.

"It doesn't act like an asteroid," said Ling Chow, Lowe's research assistant. "But when it passed the sun, it didn't have a tail, so it's probably not a comet."

"Vega could have been its original home. It came from that direction. However," Lowe drew on his unlit pipe, "Vega wasn't there when it left the area thousands of years ago."

"So, where did it come from?" the boy asked. "What is it?"

"That, my son, is the question."

Even though they couldn't explain its trajectory and inconsistent acceleration as it swung around the sun and back out into space, most astronomers thought it a natural phenomenon. A few, though, insisted it must be an alien construct and dubbed it Oumuamua, the scout, because whatever it was, it did not originate in the solar system.

Levi Lowe was one of the strongest proponents of the alien origin theory. He declared, "I think we should build a probe and chase it down."

His associates concurred. "We could reach it as early as 2047," one said, and Project Lyra was born in 2021 before the war started in Ukraine. Not that a little thing like a possible nuclear conflagration would have stopped Levi Lowe. Cancer did. Lowe, Jr. stared at the funeral picture of his father, pipe in his mouth, hat on his head, a throwback to a Norman Rockwell painting.

Ling Chow expressed his condolences as they left the memorial. Ling was now a prominent scientist himself, and Lowe had grown up to follow in his father's footsteps.

"I promised Dad I would carry on the project," Lowe said with one backward glance at the fragrant lilies festooning the flowered urn.

"We will complete it together," Ling assured him, dark eyes twinkling like a starry night.

But Lowe worried. Would they be able to decipher whatever alien signals they might receive? Stephen Hawking said if humans were inferior to aliens, contact with them may not end well for humanity. Lowe couldn't help thinking about what had happened to inferior beings when humanity came in contact with them.

As it turned out, man was his own worst enemy. The nuclear war that had been brewing ever since the bomb's invention finally erupted in 2040. The great bear swept down from the north. Dragons flew in from the east. When the bombs dropped, they looked like stars falling from the sky. The sun went black as sackcloth, and the moon turned red as blood. In the aftermath, plague, famine, and pestilence of biblical proportions came.

The western United States was uninhabitable due to radioactivity from the attack on its nuclear silos. Yet from New York south to Florida and west to Kentucky, vassals of China still subsisted. Vassals like Levi Lowe, Jr. and Ling Chow continued with the Lyra project under Chinese auspices. China wasn't worried by Hawking's prediction. After all, China had conquered the world.

In 2043, the team discovered a capsule believed to have been launched from the Oumuamua probe.

"It's heading for Earth at a speed mankind cannot achieve," Ling Chow told his team of Chinese and American astronomers.

The team kept a close watch on it, and as the capsule drew nearer, it appeared to be a living thing rather than a mechanical one. Hoping for something more complex than a mere spore that could survive in space, and for lack of a better term, Lowe called it the Interstellar Chrysalis. He said it would reach Earth by 2047, and he and Ling narrowed the arrival time to late December. They announced worldwide, prompting short-lived evangelists to decry them as false prophets.

"No telling what this . . . this thing might portend for humanity," the holy men exclaimed.

Lowe, remembering Hawking's warning, tended to agree with them. "What kind of being might metamorphosis from such a chrysalis?" he asked. "Something alien to man? A xenomorph?" Using the ebony stem of the pipe his father left him, a pipe he never filled, he indicated an artist's rendering that looked suspiciously like the alien in the movie. "Something even worse, perhaps?" His sea-green eyes flashed, adding emphasis to his words. "An entity able to combine with other lifeforms and create a supernatural hybrid?"

Jacobson Leyman, faced him down. The West China (formerly the U.S.) Communist Party added him to the team, though he hailed from the erstwhile U.K. Born some years before Ling and Lowe, he seemed a wizened addition. What he had done before joining the scientific community was a mystery. And in a world where people had become worthless commodities, he seemed to hold the strange belief that mankind still mattered.

"I think you're wrong on all counts," he told Lowe. "This chrysalis could be invaluable for humanity. It could be bringing us a cure for cancer. Or a way to conquer all diseases and infirmities. It may endow us with indestructible bodies."

Lowe began to reconsider. A cure for cancer? It had been his vision ever since cancer claimed his dad. Was this chrysalis his dream come true, or would it be a nightmare?

Before Lowe could speak, Ling Chow entered the dispute with a sensitive subject, considering the onset and outcome of World War III. "Perhaps it will provide insurmountable armament."

"Just what mankind needs," said the conflicted Lowe. "A deadlier weapon."

"An ultimate weapon could end all war," Ling countered.

Leyman confirmed it as a valid point, embracing a prince of peace. "Suppose this chrysalis is immortal, having done away with disease and disorder," he said. "Suppose it does have the ability to combine with other lifeforms. Through that union, might it not instill the secret of everlasting life in us?"

They had not come to a consensus when the crisis occurred. Tracking had the Interstellar Chrysalis aiming for Israel, totally uninhabitable by man after the holocaust. Lowe still mistrusted it, so he joined Leyman and Ling, desperately trying to signal the chrysalis. They sent diagrams of the nuclear warning sign and pictures of the devastated area.

Their efforts did not deter the Interstellar Chrysalis. It touched down in Jerusalem. That is, earthlings thought it landed there. As the chrysalis approached, clouds were only visible on the satellite feed.

Then, floating out of the clouds, came one humanoid man. He walked on the desolate plain and transformed the Kidron Valley into the melancholic beauty of Gethsemane's garden. The man did not perish in the radiation but cleansed the earth of humanity's sin and pollution. World leaders and scientists, Lowe included, backpedaled — or they would have if they had not been on their knees. They did not want to see this man. But some, like the mysterious Leyman, rejoiced. Some welcomed His Second Coming.

Bonnie B. Herrick lives in Louisville, Kentucky with her husband, daughter, granddaughter, two big dogs, and two sneaky cats. She likes to read, write, walk her dogs, and knit. Published in the Florida Writer's Association (FWA) 2016 and 2021 Collections, the FWA magazine, and the Kentucky Monthly Literary issue she also judges for a literary contest. Bonnie has been a finalist and semi-finalist for the Royal Palm Literary Awards.

The Art of Waiting

Mary Park

The things I plan won't happen right away. Slowly, steadily, surely, the time approaches when the vision will be fulfilled. If it seems slow do not despair, for these things will surely come to pass. Just be patient! They will not be overdue a single day!
Habakkuk 2:3, TLB

Habakkuk, a minor prophet, was quite concerned about the evil and corruption in Judah. He seemed to feel like the Lord wasn't doing anything about it. The Lord assured Habakkuk that He was doing something, but it would seem shocking and unbelievable. God planned to overcome evil with even more evil by bringing the Babylonians into Judah.

In Habakkuk 2:3 God explained to Habakkuk that he must wait and how long he must wait. Whatever God was going to do would happen in God's timing, which may seem slow by human standards. Habakkuk must learn patience and not be anxious about what God would do and when He would do it.

In seasons of waiting, we should also follow these instructions God gave Habakkuk.

We are all waiting for something. Perhaps you are waiting for your dream job, healing from cancer, or reconciliation of a broken relationship. You could be single, waiting to be married.

Waiting is a battle. It is difficult to wait when we can't see God working or know how long we must wait. It takes all we've got not to go ahead of God and make things happen.

During a time in my life the thing I was waiting for became an idol. Having a husband was all I could think about. When Ben came into my life, I thought God had finally answered my prayer. Ben also had children. I would have my own little family.

My happily–ever–after soon began to crumble. The relationship was unhealthy, and I needed out. I was at the end of myself. I've heard that when you come to the end of yourself, that is where God begins. God provided a way out.

When I obeyed God and broke up with Ben, God opened my eyes to the ways He had already provided for me: a wonderful family, an amazing group of friends, an awesome church, and a great place to live. Thirty-eight blessings came from one simple act of obedience. My top two blessings were seeing myself the way God sees me and developing a more intimate relationship with Him. God provided opportunities that I never would have expected — acting in the Christmas musicals at church, serving at the welcome desk, and traveling.

My latest adventure is certainly a surprise. My church did not have a singles' group, and now it does. I facilitate group. Now, for a person who never wanted to be labeled single and who disliked most singles' groups she had ever attended, this new role was certainly unexpected. God definitely has a sense of humor.

The words in Habakkuk 2:3 can be applied to both the Jewish people of Abraham's day and the Jewish people in the New Testament as they wait for the promised Messiah. They were expecting God to save them from their situation with a king, but instead, they got a lowly baby born in a manger. How could a mere human save them? Many people were disappointed. Many didn't believe that Jesus was the Messiah, and others were threatened by Him.

Sometimes, we don't know what we are waiting for until it comes. We are just like the people in Jesus' day. We live in a broken and sinful world and need saving. Jesus was the greatest provision that God could have ever given to us, to them. By dying on the cross, Jesus took the punishment for our sins upon Himself. He provided the only way to spend eternity with Him in heaven.

After God told Habakkuk what would happen, Habakkuk stopped worrying. He just waited, living with joyful anticipation.

We are to follow Habakkuk's example of waiting by praying and praising the Lord. "O Lord, now I have heard your report, and I worship you in awe for the fearful things you are going to do." (Habakkuk 3:2, TLB)

When our plans fall through, we often respond the way the people did in Jesus' time — with disappointment, disbelief, and anger toward God. It is important to remember what Jesus did for us, especially in waiting times. God's plans for us are good. We must give the control back to God because He knows what is best for us. God sees the big picture. We must wait and actively trust that the Lord will do whatever He has promised. Delay is often a way God protects us.

We may not have a choice about what we must wait for, but we can decide how we wait. To be better equipped for knowing how to wait, consider all the ways God has provided for you in the past. Then, ask these two questions. Has God always provided for me how I expected? Did God provide what was best for me at that time?

Remember, "Trust in the Lord with all your heart, and do not lean on your own understanding. In all your ways acknowledge Him, and He will make straight your paths" (Prov. 3:5–6, ESV).

Mary Park is a recently retired elementary school teacher. In this new chapter of her life, Mary would like to use the gifts God has given her in writing, speaking, acting, and storytelling to bring Him glory. Mary lives in Barrie, Ontario with her playful and energetic cat, Jenga.

The Lord Will Provide

Darcy Hicks

*And Abraham named that place The LORD Will Provide, so today
it is said, "It will be provided on the Lord's mountain."*
Genesis 22:14, CSB

Have you ever been through a difficult time, and then
suddenly God answered your prayer or moved in a special
way that you knew it was His provision? If you are
breathing, you likely have experienced painful situations.
Sometimes, those seasons come and go quickly; other times,
they seem to drag on forever.

One difficult memory for me is when my husband was
chronically ill for several years with no real answers. He
endured tests and more tests, multiple emergency room
visits, doctor visits, and yet it seemed his condition only
worsened.

And just when we thought we were facing a long-term
diagnosis that projected a continual decline in his health and
physical abilities, a new surgeon's diagnosis changed
everything. I have often thought about how that one doctor's
visit transformed our future. Our life seemed dim and his
prognosis poor when God unexpectedly provided an answer
to our prayers that breathed hope back into our lives. God's
provision can often come when we least expect it and with a
bounty we don't deserve.

We can find a good example of this in the story of
Abraham and Isaac (Genesis 22:1–19). Abraham had waited
decades for God to fulfill the promise of a son. But when

Isaac was older, God commanded Abraham to do the unthinkable and sacrifice his son. Abraham took Isaac to the mountain, and preparing to comply with God's command, he raised the knife to take his son's life. But God, seeing Abraham's heart and obedience, sent an angel to stop him and provided an animal sacrifice in his son's place. Abraham, praising God, named the place where it occurred, "The Lord will provide."

As hard as it is to imagine sacrificing his one-and-only son, Abraham obeyed God even though there did not appear to be any other means of sacrifice besides his son. Isaac had even begun to question his father, "Where is the lamb for the offering?" to which Abraham replied, "God will provide for himself the lamb for a burnt offering, my son" (v. 7–8). Abraham's belief that God would provide the sacrifice through Isaac or another means proved his trust in God.

During a time in my husband's illness, I had to lay it down and accept God's will for our lives, even if it meant my husband would never get well. Despite the tears and the railing against this plan, peace came when I said, "God, your will be done." And while the answers didn't come instantly, God, in His perfect time, pointed us in a new direction for my husband's healing, through that one doctor's visit.

I am so thankful for that unexpected answer because at other times, God did not deliver a miracle answer or change a situation. But I can still attest that He is Jehovah Jireh, my Provider. He provides peace. He provides love. He provides comfort. He provides answers. And He provides everything we need to endure challenging times, even when we do not get our miracle.

Are there places in your life that you, too, could name "The Lord will provide"? Or are there situations or loved ones that you need to lay down and put in God's hands, trusting that He will provide for your every need according to His riches in glory (Philippians 4:19)?

I pray both you and I would have the faith and obedience of Abraham to know that He is the Lord God, our provider, in every situation and circumstance.

Darcy Hicks lives in Northwest Florida with her husband and children. She encourages others in their faith through writing and speaking. Connect with Darcy through her blog at darcyhicks.com.

Living Parables of Central Florida, of which EABooks Publishing is a division, supports Christian charities providing for the needs of their communities. Ministries are encouraged to join hands and hearts with like-minded charities to better meet unmet needs in their communities.

Mission Statement

To empower start up, nonprofit organizations financially, spiritually, and with sound business knowledge to participate successfully as a responsible 501(c)3 organization that contributes to the Kingdom work of God.

Made in the USA
Middletown, DE
18 September 2024

60577756R00053